Family Favorites
The Best of Tom Chapin

For information about Tom Chapin, contact:
Sundance Music
100 Cedar Street, Suite B-19
Dobbs Ferry, NY 10522 USA
Phone/Fax 914-674-0247
info@tomchapin.com
www.tomchapin.com

Teachers, please visit www.tomchapin.com for song lyrics and classroom activities.

Cover photo by Jim Graham
Photo by Bonnie Chapin
Illustrations by Lynn Whisnant Reiser and Tom Chapin

This book was approved by Tom Chapin.

Cherry Lane Music Company
Director of Publications/Project Editor: Mark Phillips
Publications Coordinator: Gabrielle Fastman

ISBN 1-57560-845-6

Visit our website at www.cherrylane.com

TOM CHAPIN

An American childhood would be incomplete without the music of Tom Chapin. Through 30 years and many award-winning recordings, Chapin has entertained, amused, and enlightened audiences of all ages with life-affirming original songs told in a sophisticated array of musical styles.

A pioneer in the field of children's music, Chapin and his collaborators (John Forster, Michael Mark, and Jon Cobert) have created classic family CDs, crafting an ever-expanding body of music aimed at the post-toddler, pre-teen set, and their parents. These songs are full of ideas, yet, while many impart a message, the overall tone remains light and fun. Teachers throughout North America have incorporated Chapin's songs into their curriculum, finding them accessible and adaptable to classroom study and interaction.

Billboard magazine calls Chapin "the best family artist around." The *New York Times* calls him "one of the great personalities in contemporary folk music."

Tom has been showered with awards, including multiple Grammys for Best Spoken Word Album for Children and several additional Grammy nominations for Best Musical Album for Children.

Cherry Lane is proud to present this collection of *Family Favorites,* songs that Tom and his band sing at almost every concert, songs that have become part of America's musical landscape.

DISCOGRAPHY

The songs contained in this songbook can be found on the following Tom Chapin recordings:

SONG	CD
Alphabet Soup	*Moonboat*
The Backwards Birthday Party	*Zag Zig*
Cousins	*Mother Earth*
Family Tree	*Family Tree*
Good Garbage	*Mother Earth, This Pretty Planet*
Great Big Words	*Billy the Squid*
Happy Birthday	*Moonboat, Great Big Fun*
Library Song	*Moonboat*
A Mozart Duet	*In My Hometown*
R-E-C-Y-C-L-E	*Zag Zig, This Pretty Planet*
This Pretty Planet	*Family Tree, This Pretty Planet*
Together Tomorrow	*Family Tree, Great Big Fun*
Uh Oh, Accident	*Family Tree, Great Big Fun*
What Is a Didjeridoo?	*Around the World and Back Again*

Alphabet Soup

Words and Music by
Michael Mark and Tom Chapin

In April 1990, I got a letter and a book of photos from Caroline Johnson,
a teacher at Riverfield Country Day School in Tulsa, Oklahoma:

Dear Tom:

The fun we had with "Alphabet Soup!" Each child was
assigned a letter and, on cards of cut poster board, drew the
food to go with that letter. During music, they sat around the
edge of the rug and, as each letter came around, he'she rose
on his knees and held the letter aloft."Let's go 'round and
sing it again . . ." looked really impressive, akin to the card
section at a baseball game. *So much incorporated into one
song . . . alphabet, art, language, nutrition, rhyming, rhythm,
listening skills and anticipation, even a little math as we
calculated "sets of three" for the photo shoot.*

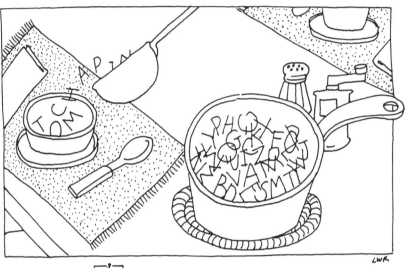

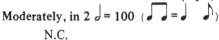

(Spoken:) Now gath-er round chil-dren. It's time for a treat. Din-ner time's com-in'.

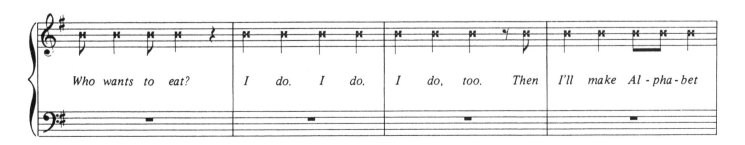

Who wants to eat? I do. I do. I do, too. Then I'll make Al-pha-bet

4

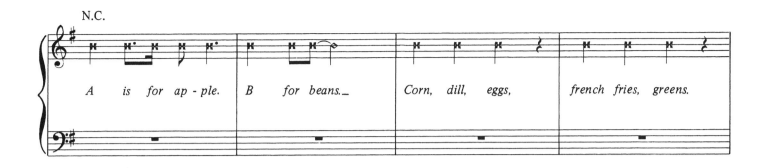

A is for ap-ple. B for beans.__ Corn, dill, eggs, french fries, greens.

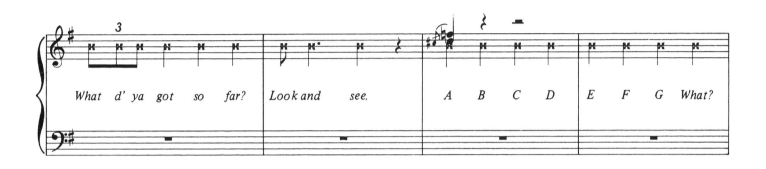

What d' ya got so far? Look and see. A B C D E F G What?

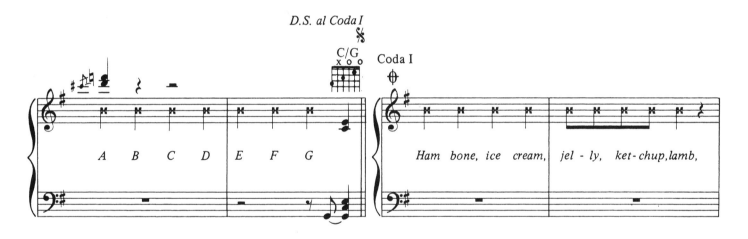

A B C D E F G

Ham bone, ice cream, jel-ly, ket-chup, lamb,

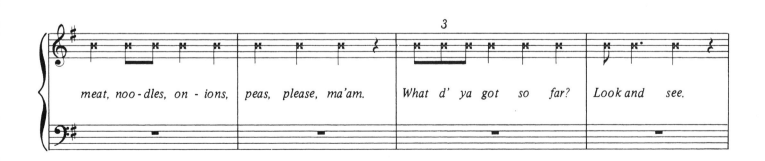

meat, noo-dles, on-ions, peas, please, ma'am. What d' ya got so far? Look and see.

5

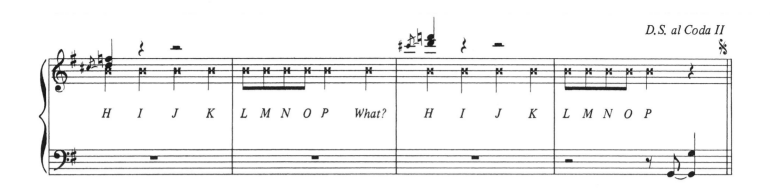

H I J K L M N O P   What?   H I J K L M N O P

Coda II

Quince, rad - ish, salt, tur - nips,   u - ni - corn horn,   veal chop, wa - ter-mel-on... u - ni - corn horn?

Play my xy - lo - phone while it's stew - in',   let's put yams in. Let's put you in! A

big zuc - chi - ni when no one's look - in'.   Now we've got__ the whole al - pha - bet cook - in'.

6

Al - pha - bet Soup   could - n't be bet - ter. Let's say the whole thing let - ter by let - ter:

A B C D E F G   H I J K   L M N O P

Q R S   T U V   W (dou-ble U) X   Y and Z

Let's go round and   sing it a - gain._Then   pass   me an S - P - O - O - N.

Coda III

Can't get e - nough of that Al - pha - bet Soup.   Al - pha-bet Soup.

7

The Backwards Birthday Party

We've had lots of great birthday parties at our house, but never one quite like this.

Words and Music by
John Forster and Tom Chapin

9

Additional Lyrics

2. We ate the birthday cake first, which stirred up quite a fuss.
We blindfolded the donkey, and he pinned the tail on us.
The treasure hunt went nowhere, but no one was depressed.
'Cause I wrapped up all my presents, and gave one to every guest. *(To Chorus)*

3. The clock was running backward, struck three then two then one.
My party, it was winding down before it had begun.
I said, "Hello, it's time to go!" and pushed them out the door,
And I was one year younger than I'd been the day before. *(To Chorus)*

Cousins

There's nothing more exhilarating than a stampede of wild cousins.

Words and Music by
John Forster and Tom Chapin

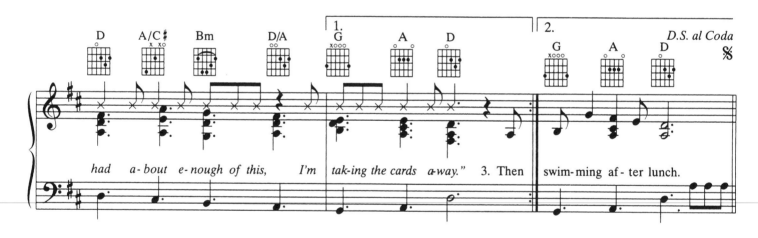

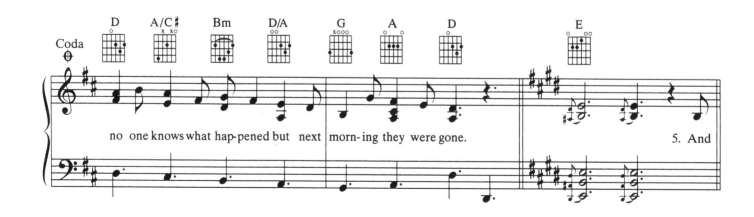

then at break-fast ba-by Gail went back-ward in her chair.

6. *See additional lyrics*

"Mik-ey pushed me!" "Was-n't me!" "Was!" "Was not, I swear!" Then

Mik-ey threw a muf-fin, hit-ting Bil-ly on the bean, 'twas the

most gi-gan-tic food fight this world has ev-er seen.

Chorus

Cous-ins, cous-ins, here come the boys. Bed-lam, may-hem,

Repeat and fade

Additional Lyrics

3. Then Butchie went and fell on a rake and bled all over the floor.
   They stitched him up and gave him a shot and Butchie was back for more.
   He ate a hero sandwich and he drank a quart of punch.
   Then he disobeyed the doctor and went swimming after lunch. *(To Chorus)*

4. Late that night we bedded down and began the pillow fight
   That broke the big aquarium the mirror and the light.
   We swept the glass and saved the fish and put 'em in the john.
   Well, no one knows what happened but next morning they were gone. *(To Coda)*

6. Then Uncle Hugh said, "Time to go, we gotta get out of here."
   It took them half the afternoon to pack up all their gear.
   And when they piled into the car Aunt Bess was full of woe.
   "Bye-bye!" "So long!" "See ya!" "Bye!" "Bye-bye!" "Bye!" "Yo!" *(To Chorus)*

Family Tree

Words and Music by
John Forster and Tom Chapin

It's fun to really make a family tree. Get a big sheet of paper and write down every member of your family you can think of: mothers, fathers, sisters, brothers, uncles, cousins, grandparents. Ask the oldest ones to tell you about other members you never knew. Then you can draw up your official family tree with every "branch" and "twig" and "leaf."

Moderate 2, with a bounce ♩ = 108

1. Be - fore the days of Jel - lo lived a
2.3. See additional lyrics

deep down in ___ his - to - ry, from my great - great -

last time: {grand - dad - dy / grand - moth - er} reach - in' up to me; ___ we're a green and

grow - ing ___ fam - 'ly tree.

1.2.

2. My

3.

4. The folks in Ma - da - gas - car aren't the

same as in A - las - kar; __ they got dif - f'rent foods, __ dif - f'rent moods __ and

dif - f'rent col - ored skin. You may have a

dif - f'rent name but un - der - neath we're much the same. You're prob - a - bly __ my

D.S. al Coda

cous - in, _____ and the whole world is our kin. We're a

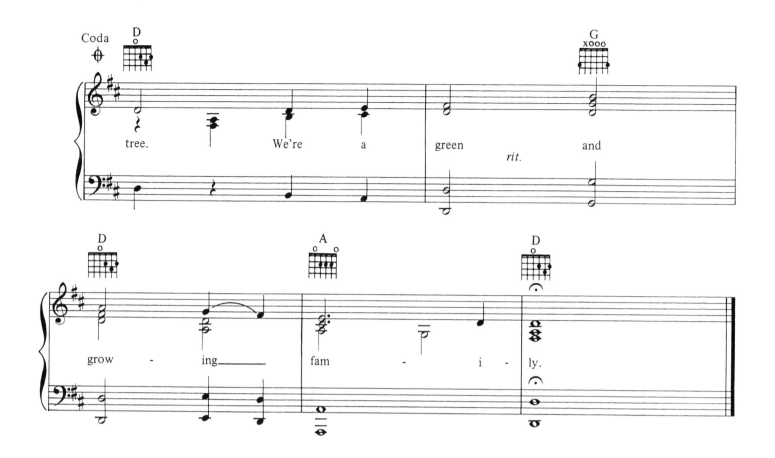

Additional Lyrics

2. My grandpa came from Russia; my grandma came from Prussia;
   They met in Nova Scotia, had my dad in Tennessee.
   Then they moved to Yokahama, where Daddy met my mama.
   Her dad's from Alabama and her mom's part Cherokee. *(To Chorus)*

3. One fine day I may go to Tierra del Fuego.
   Perhaps I'll meet my wife there and we'll move to Timbuktu.
   And our kid will be bilingual, and though she may stay single,
   She could, of course, co-mingle with the king of Katmandu. *(To Chorus)*

4. The folks in Madagascar aren't the same as in Alaskar;
   They got different foods, different moods and diffrerent colored skin.
   You may have a different name, but underneath we're much the same.
   You're probably my cousin and the whole world is our kin. *(To Chorus)*

Good Garbage

Words and Music by
John Forster and Tom Chapin

Moderately fast

I had a tur-key din-ner, threw the
sty-ro-foam is bad, it lasts a

bones a - way. They hauled them to the coun-ty dump with-out de - lay. By the
thou-sand years. A pack-ing pea-nut's born and nev-er dis-ap-pears. So

smells bad to your nose. Bad gar - bage grows and grows and grows.

1. A7 Gar - bage is s'posed to de - com - pose. D

2. A Gar - bage,

G# 4fr. gar - bage, A gar - bage is A7 s'posed to de - com - pose. D

CLYNN REISER 1992

Great Big Words

*As we get older the words we comprehend and utilize get more precise and grandiose. You could use
a dictionary or thesaurus to substitute your own massive ideograms for the ones in this composition.*

Words and Music by
Michael Mark and Tom Chapin

Brightly (with a Salsa feel)

Tacet

La la, la la la la la, la la la!

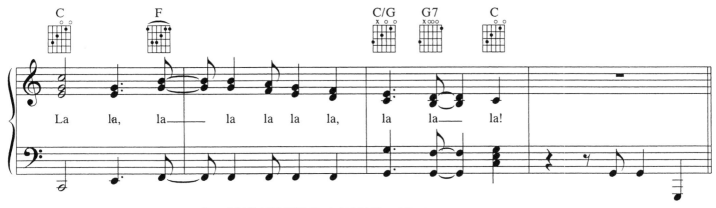

La la, la la la la la, la la la!

1. When I was a lit - tle kid,___ a "di - min - u - tive ju - ve - nile,"
2.3. *See additional lyrics*

___ I liked my folks to read___ to me,___ I was an

"ea - ger bib - li - o - phile." Now, I love words for how___

___ they sound___ and how___ they "com - mu - ni - cate."___ Per -

haps I should ex - plain___ my - self, that is, "e - lu - ci - date."___

was "u-nique"; peo - ple thought I was one of a kind. ___ When my

word of the day ___ was "dis - tin - gué," ___ peo - ple said I was ver - y re -

fined. But they look at me like I'm an a - li - en, when I

say things like "ses - qui - pe - da - li - an." ___ But what, me wor - ry? I

can't go wrong ___ with a word that's a foot and one ___ half long.

Great   big   words,____   I

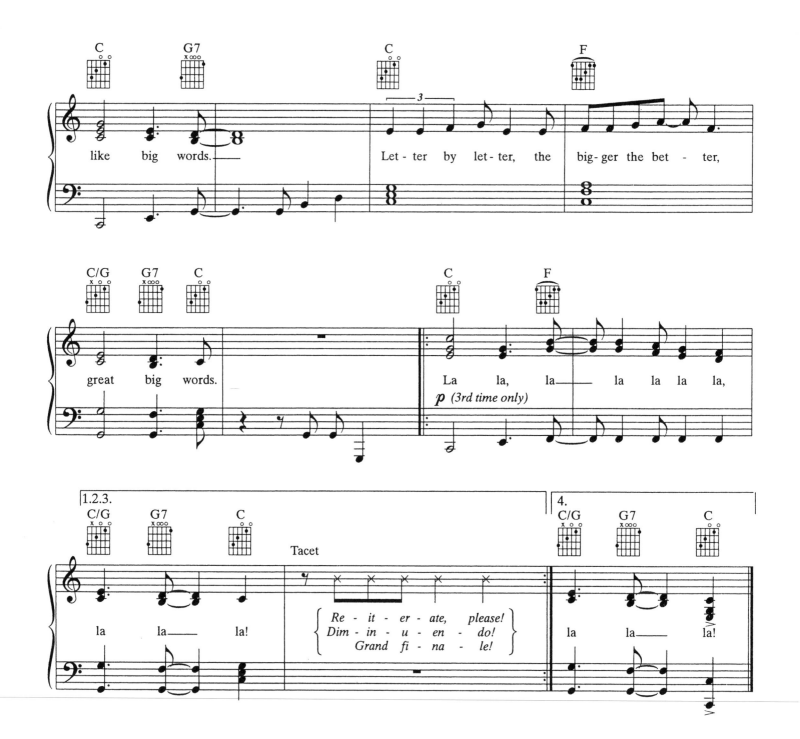

Additional Lyrics

2. Now, maybe you're "adept" at sports or "excellent" at school.
Maybe you're "vainglorious," which means you think you're cool.
But give me a "massive ideogram," a big word to make my point.
When you can "verbalize" yourself, you can really rock the joint.

2nd Chorus:
Great big words, I like big words.
I get a thrill out of every syllable,
Great big words. *(To Bridge)*

3. Big words are "prodigious terms," now don't they sound delicious?
They impress your teachers, confuse your parents, and make your friends suspicious.
But that's okay, we'll start a trend that soon will sweep the nation;
The hyper-linguistic polysyllabic speech association.

3rd Chorus:
Great big words, I like big words.
No extra charge if it's very large,
Those great big words. *(To Coda)*

Happy Birthday

Lyrics Traditional

"Merry Widow Waltz" by Franz Lehar
Arranged by John Forster and Tom Chapin

The tune is the famous "Merry Widow Waltz" by Franz Lehar. We don't know who made up these words, but they fit perfectly. When your birthday comes, why don't you sing this one for a change of pace?

Moderately ♩.= 54

Hap - py birth - day, hap - py birth - day, we

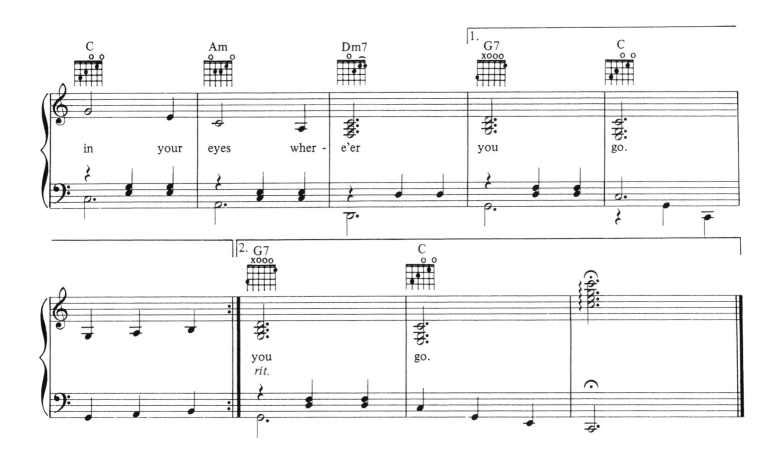

in your eyes wher - e'er you go.

1. G7 ... C

2. G7 ...
you *rit.*
C ...
go.

Library Song

Words and Music by
Michael Mark and Tom Chapin

''I like books and they like me . . .'' When we read a good book, the characters do seem to come to life, at least in our imaginations. Are there characters that you've read about that you'd like to meet in real life? Which favorites of yours did we leave out? Draw a picture of your library with book characters coming alive. (By the way, Mrs. Parker is a real librarian at Michael Mark's library in Valley Cottage, New York.)

Freely

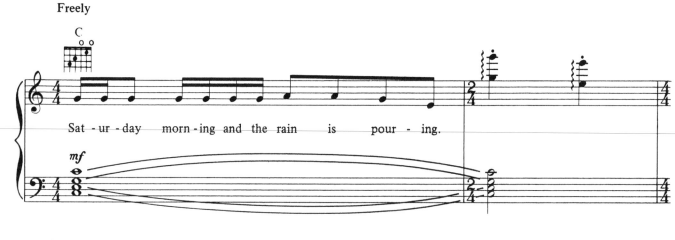

Sat - ur - day morn - ing and the rain is pour - ing.

Dad worked late last night, he's in there snor - ing.

Same old stuff on T - V, bor - ing.

Moderately Fast ♩ = 96

So what if I can't go out and play, I know what I'll do to-day.

I'm going down to the li-brar-y,

pick-ing out a book, check it in, check it out. Gon-na say hi to the

dic-tion-ar-y, pick-ing out a book, check it in, check it out.

3rd time to Coda I;
4th time to Coda II

Now I like books and they like me, so when I go to the
Sleep-ing Beau-ty yawned and said, "I'll come when I get

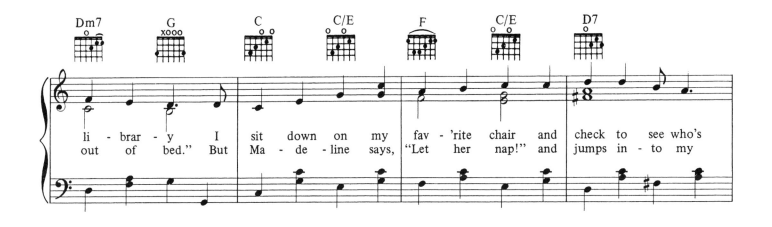

li - brar - y I sit down on my fav - 'rite chair and check to see who's
out of bed." But Ma - de - line says, "Let her nap!" and jumps in - to my

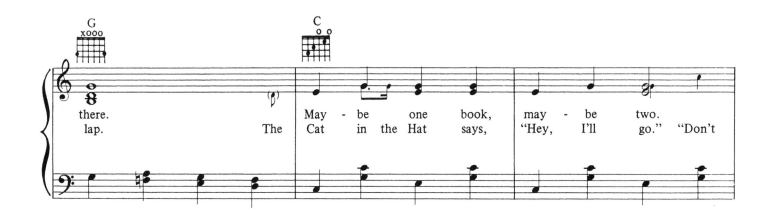

there. The May - be one book, may - be two.
lap. Cat in the Hat says, "Hey, I'll go." "Don't

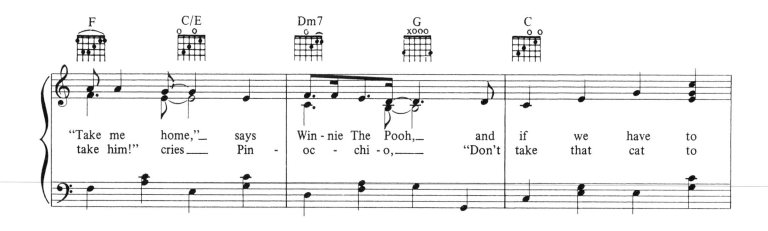

"Take me home,"__ says Win - nie The Pooh,__ and if we have to
take him!" cries__ Pin - oc - chi - o,__ "Don't take that cat to

2nd time D.S. al Coda I

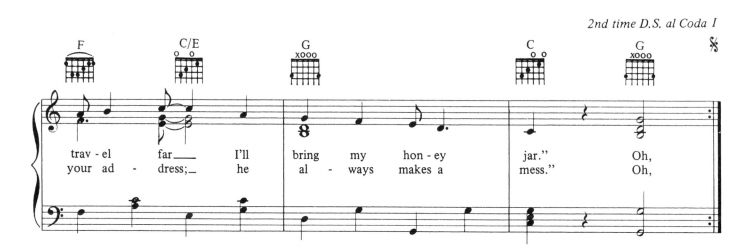

trav - el far__ I'll bring my hon - ey jar." Oh,
your ad - dress;__ he al - ways makes a mess." Oh,

Coda I

Am

Em

Dm

Mis - sus   Par - ker's   back   be - hind   the   check - out   desk   to -

C   Dm7   C   D7

day.   The   Chesh - ire   Cat   jumps   on   her   head   and   says,   "Let's

G   Am   Em7

play!"   But   Miss - us   P.   says,   "Good - ness,   are   you

Dm   C/E   F   C   C/E

sure   you   want   all   these?"   "Oh   yes!"   we   shout   to -

F

D.S. al Coda II

%

geth - er.   She says, *(Whispered:)* "Shhh!   Qui - et   *please!"*

p

39

Coda II

The Sev-en Dwarfs be-gin to shout,__ "Say,

take us with__ you. Check us out!" Then Cin-der-el-la

gets her gown and Ba-bar grabs his crown. Then

Cur-ious George swings from the shelf. A-long comes Moth-er Goose her-self.

Out the door__ we danced and sang. The whole li-brar-y rang. Oh,

A Mozart Duet

*Playing a great piece of music is not easy. It takes concentration,
practice, and a kind of collaboration with its author.*

Words and Music by
Jon Cobert, Michael Mark
and Tom Chapin
Sonata III by W.A. Mozart

Mo - zart piece a - gain. Next month is the

big re - cit - al and I have to get it right by then.

(Sigh) This sec - ond part is

much   too dif - fi - cult for an - y kid to play.

Fin - gers just weren't meant to move this fast. Who wrote this tur - key an - y -

way? *(Mozart:)* "I did. It's not dif - fi - cult, a

sim - ple scale in C. I'm Wolf - gang A - ma -

de - us Mo - zart and I could have played this at age three. *Try it again."*

(Me:) Ugh! *(Mozart:)* "There's no need to

get dis - cour - aged; it takes time to learn to play.

Prac - tice it a lit - tle slow - er. You must let your fin - gers lead the

big   re - cit - al   and   it   filled   the   li - brar - y.   The

crowd   grew   hushed   and   I   was   nerv - ous,   un - til   Mo - zart   turned   and   said   to

me,   *(Mozart:)* "I'm   ver - y   proud   of   how   you've   worked.   Now,

show   them   how   you   play!"   *(Me:)* I   sat   down   at   the

48

grand pi-an-o and I let my fin-gers lead the way.

R-E-C-Y-C-L-E

How to make the recycling concept interesting and fun for kids? Michael and I decided to tell the story from a stegosaurus' point of view.

Words and Music by
Michael Mark and Tom Chapin

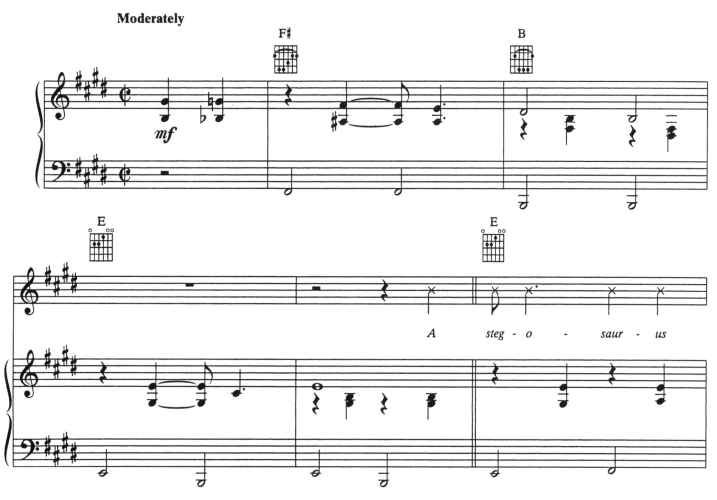

in the for-est munch-ing on some hay lay

down to snooze in a bed of ooze—— and sad-ly passed a-

way. Her bod-y changed and re-ar-ranged—— as she

sank be-neath the soil, and o-ver time she

turned to slime,___ and then she turned to oil.

So she

dis - ap - pears___ for a   jil - lion years till   fi - n'lly she is
late___ Ju - ras - sic___   it's fan - tas - sic   how our di - no
di - no - saur___ could___   see us pour - ing   or - ange juice this

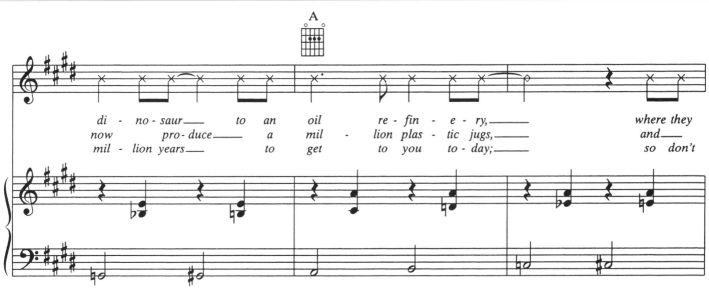

This Pretty Planet

Words and Music by
John Forster and Tom Chapin

Here's another round, a round for the round earth. The easiest way to learn it is in sections: divide a group in thirds and each learn one of the three parts. Can you picture the earth as a nursery? A space ship? Imagine you're an astronaut in space looking down on our giant ball of a planet. Draw a picture of what it might look like.

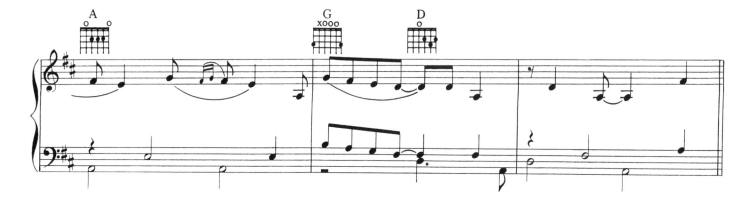

*Beginning 2nd time, sing as a round with each voice entering where indicated.

Together Tomorrow

Words and Music by
John Forster and Tom Chapin

Saying goodbye is one of the hardest things we have
to learn how to do. Maybe this song will help to
remind you that endings are also beginnings.

*Sing harmony (small notes) 3rd time only.

Uh Oh, Accident

Words and Music by
John Forster and Tom Chapin

After you learn this song you might have fun making up extra verses for it. "Slipped on a pickle and took a spill... or, "Tripped on the trash with a dreadful bump..." Get the idea? Then you could illustrate the verses.

66

What Is a Didjeridoo?

I love not only the sounds, but the names, of musical instruments. Like balalaika, bouzouki, ukulele, oud, hurdy-gurdy and yes, the didjeridoo.

Words and Music by
Michael Mark and Tom Chapin

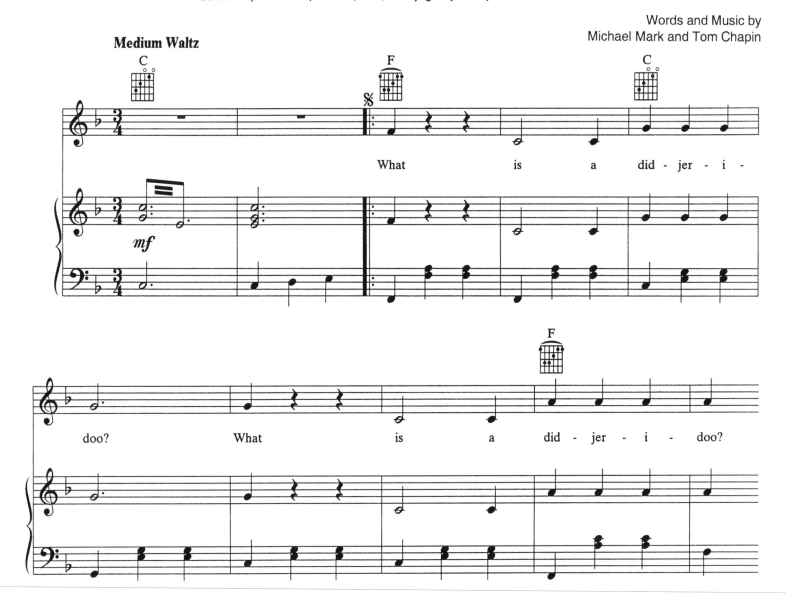

What is a did - jer - i - doo? What is a did - jer - i - doo?

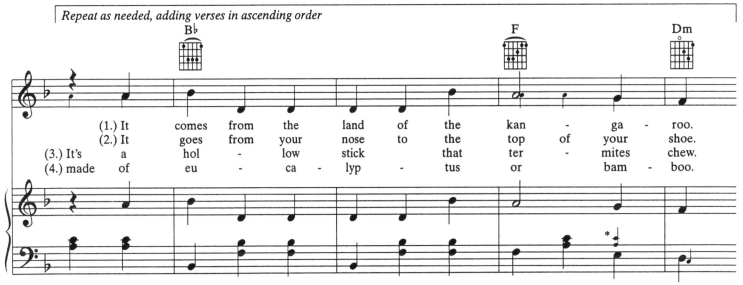

Repeat as needed, adding verses in ascending order

(1.) It comes from the land of the kan - ga - roo.
(2.) It goes from your nose to the top of your shoe.
(3.) It's a hol - low stick that ter - mites chew.
(4.) made of eu - ca - lyp - tus or bam - boo.

*Substitute cue notes for lines 2, 3, and 4.

But what does a did-jer-i-doo do?

What does a did-jer-i-doo?

I learned all a-bout the bou-zou-ki from a
In Ha-wa-ii I heard u-ku-le-le from a
I know 'bout the bal-a-lai-ka from a
A Ca-rib-be-an cap-tain named Mon-go played me